Covenant Discipleship Parents' Handbook

Covenant Discipleship Parents' Handbook

The Handbook for a new sort of Communicant's Class

Helping Students Understand Faith, Theology, and the Church

By Richard L. Burguet & J.E. Eubanks, Jr.

Copyright ©2000 by Richard L. Burguet and J.E. Eubanks, Jr.

All rights reserved. No part of this book may be used or reproduced in any manner whatsoever without written permission, except in the case of brief quotations embodied in critical articles or reviews.

Published 2008; Reprinted 2020

ISBN 978-1-937063-00-9

Dedicated to our covenant families:

Burguets:
   Anne, Iain, Elizabeth, Suzanna, Mary Claire, Katie, John, Johnathan, and Mackenzie.

Eubanks's:
   Marcie, Jack, Molly, Abbey, and Caroline.

Thank you for your constant love and support.

Table of Contents

Introduction—Welcome! 1
Lesson 1: Faith and Its Foundation 5
Section 1: What is this faith stuff? 6
Section 2: The foundations of faith 8
Section 3: The Bible— a strong foundation 9
Section 4: The Bible, part 2 10
Section 5: How God relates to us 11
Lesson 1 Summary 12
Lesson 2: Understanding Your Faith 13
Section 1: God's relationship to the world, continued: God's righteousness 14
Section 2: God's relationship to the world, part 3: mercy and grace 15
Section 3: Jesus OUR salvation 16
Section 4: What is a testimony? 18
Section 5: Your testimony 19
Lesson 2 Summary 20
Lesson 3: Basic Training 21
Section 1: God's covenants with man 22
Section 2: God's covenants with man, part 2 23
Section 3: God's covenants with man, part 3 25
Section 4: Justification 27
Section 5: Sanctification 28
Lesson 3 Summary 29
Lesson 4: Why Do We Baptize Babies? 31
Section 1: Predestination 32
Section 2: The Sacraments, part 1 34
Section 3: The Sacraments, part 2 36
Lesson 4 Summary 38
Lesson 5: The Church 39
Section 1: The church universal and the church particular 40
Section 2: The church ministers to others 41
Section 3: The church ministers to you 43
Lesson 5 Summary 44
Lesson 6: Getting Down to Business 45
Section 1: Our denomination, other denominations 46
Section 2: The officers of the church 48
Section 3: The officers of the church, continued. 50
Section 4: Church governing and membership 52
Lesson 6 Summary 53

Introduction—Welcome!

So, you're the parent of a Communicant's Class member! That's a very exciting position to be in—and it's also a very important position. In the Presbyterian Church in America (PCA), we take your part in this process very seriously, and we hope that you do, too.

You may be in one of a variety of different stages of church membership: you may be a long-time member of the Church, and your child is a "covenant" child; you may be fairly new to the church, but still a member; you may be entering a new members' class even now; or you may not be a member of the church, but your child wants to be. Any of these stages is fine, but we'll make two assumptions throughout this book—that you are a professing Christian, and that you are (or soon will be) a church member. If either of these is not true, please talk to your Pastor about your circumstances, and how the process might be amended to accommodate them.

A few words about the class...

There are a lot of questions that come with the possibility of taking your child through a Communicant's Class. Why is this process important—can't he/she simply join the church? Does my child need to be a certain age? What will he/she learn through this class or material? What role do I play in this process?

To be sure, the only requirement that we can biblically make of any person is that they be able to give a credible profession of faith, or as the PCA's *Book of Church Order* puts it: they must have "a profession of faith in Christ, have been baptized, and have been admitted by the Session to the Lord's Table." But beyond that, many believe that it is important that a child who wishes to join the church should understand the commitment that they are making, and the nature of the institution to which they are making that commitment. With that in mind, we have designed this curriculum for a three-fold purpose:

1. To give certainty to the profession of faith that the child might make and solid understanding of the faith they profess;
2. To educate the child about the church and its ministry, basic theology, leadership, and role in their lives; and
3. To provide an opportunity for parents to interact with their children about these important aspects of life.

Therefore, it is our belief that, within reason, there should be no age limit or requirement for church membership, nor for participation in a Communicant's Class. We feel that any child that can understand the Gospel and make a profession of saving faith in Jesus Christ can also understand the important aspects of the church that they will be learning through this material.

That is where you come in—your role is the most significant part of the whole process. As a parent, ministry to your child begins with you; you, not the local church, are primarily responsible for the direct spiritual oversight and education of your children. The local church community takes only a distant second place in this role. This means that you bear most of the burden not only for raising your child, but also for nurturing their faith and encouraging spiritual growth. Many churches have youth ministry or children's ministry programs and staff, but these exist to complement your nurturing, and to offer a support system and resource center for you—not as a replacement of your obligation and duty.

Because of this, we have chosen the name "Covenant Discipleship" for this Communicants' Class curriculum. Through the family covenant, you are raising your child or children as disciples to be a part of the church, and this class is just one step in that process.

How it will work...

This material is designed to be used as a nine-lesson class; however, you may feel the need to take a different pace with the curriculum, be it faster or slower—this is one of the very reasons it is designed the way it is. The first six lessons will be done at your own pace at home—we encourage you to be as involved in the process as you can (just don't give them the answers!). These lessons can be broken down into three categories, with two lessons for each: Faith, Theology, and Church.

Here is the basic schedule of the nine-lesson Covenant Discipleship Class:	
Lesson 1	Faith and Its Foundations: What is Faith and Why Have It?
Lesson 2	Understanding Your Faith: Up Close and Personal
Lesson 3	Basic Training: a Look at the Basics of What We Believe
Lesson 4	Why Do We Baptize Babies? And Other Good Questions…
Lesson 5	The Church: Isn't It Just a Building?
Lesson 6	Getting Down to Business: the Organization of the Church
Lesson 7	Faith and You: Review of Lessons 1 & 2
Lesson 8	What Presbyterians Believe: Review of Lessons 3 & 4
Lesson 9	We Are the Church Together: Review of Lessons 5 & 6

The last three lessons will be done in a classroom setting, perhaps during the Sunday School hour or in a small-group style context. These lessons will be taught by a Pastor or Ruling Elder, and will be a review of the material done in each of the three categories. While you are not required to attend these classes, you are welcome to do so.

This book is the parents' edition of the workbook your child has been given. It doesn't have the answers per-se, but it will give you a guide of what your child should understand at the end of each week. A copy of all of the material that your child's workbook contains is included in this book; your guide will be inset in boxes, and in a different style of type. The material is broken down into five sections per lesson, plus a summary, so that you could (for example) do one section each weekday and review over the weekend; if you prefer to do it all in one sitting, it will probably take close to two hours.

Also, there are additional resources recommended for some of the more difficult material; a list of these has been provided to your church with the suggestion that they obtain copies to make them available for your use. You will want to have a copy of the *Westminster Confession of Faith* and the *Westminster Shorter Catechism* available; these documents are the core of our denomination's statements of belief, and we will refer to them frequently through this book. Speak with your Pastor or Elder to find out what else is available to you.

This will be an exciting time for you, and it is our prayer and hope that it furthers or develops opportunities for you to interact with your child!

Lesson 1: Faith and Its Foundation

What Is Faith, and Why Have It?

In the first lesson, we'll look at what faith is, and how it is developed. We'll also look at the "foundations" of faith—what makes a person's faith believable and strong. And we'll talk about the Bible, and begin to look at how God relates to man.

Psalm 127
A SONG OF ASCENTS, OF SOLOMON.
¹Unless the LORD builds the house,
They labor in vain who build it;
Unless the LORD guards the city,
The watchman keeps awake in vain.
²It is vain for you to rise up early,
To retire late,
To eat the bread of painful labors;
For He gives to His beloved even in his sleep.
³Behold, children are a gift of the LORD,
The fruit of the womb is a reward.
⁴Like arrows in the hand of a warrior,
So are the children of one's youth.
⁵How blessed is the man whose quiver is full of them;
They will not be ashamed
When they speak with their enemies in the gate.

Section 1: What is this faith stuff?

So, What is faith? In the Bible, Hebrews chapter 11, verse 1 tells us. Look that up, and copy it here:

> **What is faith?**
> In this section we simply want to reinforce the students' understanding of what faith is, and the need for it. You should go over this material carefully with them, because their understanding of this will influence how they approach the rest of the material. You may also want to go to the Westminster Shorter Catechism question # 86 for additional study. If you do not have a copy of the Westminster Confession of Faith and the Shorter Catechism, or would like additional materials on studying the Catechism with your family see The Pastor or an Elder.

Now, what does this mean? Re-write this verse in words that describe faith as it applies to you. You might want to discuss it with your parents before you're finished.

> Parents, this is a good opportunity to interact with your students about what faith is. Two points of emphasis stand out here:
> 1. Faith is not something you do, but something you believe.
> 2. Faith always has an object, and what the object of someone's faith is will be just as important as whether they have faith.

That same chapter of Hebrews discusses a lot of people who are called "heroes of the faith" in the Bible. How did these people show their faith, and why was it important for them? Discuss some of them with your parents, and write down what you discuss.

Abel (Genesis 4:3-15):

Enoch (Genesis 5:21-24):

Noah (Genesis 6:9-7:22):

Abraham (Genesis 12:1-5; 21:1-7; 22:1-19):

Isaac (Genesis 27:1-39):

Jacob (Genesis 48:8-22):

Joseph (Genesis 50:24-26):

> **Heroes of the Faith:**
> Your student does not need to do this exercise for all of the names and verses listed; let them choose how many they want to do, but encourage them to at least look at three or four. Also they will probably need your help in understanding the link between faith and the action taken in the verses for some of the more difficult selections. Encourage your students to do at least one of the more difficult ones, and use this opportunity to discuss the difference between a faith that is active in guiding one's life and a lifeless, ineffective faith. See faith and works in James 2:14-26 ; Philippians 2:12-13 and other passages.

Moses' parents (Exodus 2:1,2):

Moses (Exodus 2:11-15; 12:31-33; 12:1-16):

Israelites (Exodus 13:17-14:31):

Joshua- Walls of Jericho (Joshua 5:13-6:27):

Rahab (Joshua 2:1-24):

How does the Bible define faith? How do the examples in the Bible demonstrate for us faith in God? Why is faith important for us? Discuss these questions with your parents.

> When we ask questions such as this one ("what do you think" questions), there is no right or wrong answer. Encourage your student that what they think is important, even if they don't believe they have the "right" answer. This will be another opportunity for discussion about what your student believes. (There will be MANY opportunities for discussion with them through the course of this curriculum!)

Section 2: The foundations of faith

A lot of people believe in a lot of different things; some people have faith in other religious beliefs, like Judaism (the Jewish religion) or Islam (the Muslim religion). Others believe in things like ghosts, witchcraft, or reincarnation— not exactly organized religions, but still significantly different beliefs from Christianity.
It is very important that we understand why our faith is valid, and why it is believable. In getting this understanding, we'll also begin to see why other religious beliefs do not have as much foundation as Christianity.

Read Matthew 7:24-27. What do these verses say about the importance of a strong foundation for faith?

What do you think makes Christianity a faith with a strong foundation?

> **A strong foundation:**
> Talk with your students about other religions (and non-religious sects and cults), and discuss with them the important differences between those beliefs and Christianity. We have a number of resources on other religions, cults and philosophies that we will be glad to help you use in this way. This section should be more discussion and thought-processing than some of the others.

Covenant Discipleship Student's Workbook

Section 3: The Bible— a strong foundation

The Bible is the foundation for Christianity— and it is a strong one. As Christians, we give the Bible a lot of attention and emphasis, because of what we believe about it.

What do we believe about the Bible? List some things that you think Christians believe about the Bible.

What does the Bible say about itself? Look up the following sets of verses, and write down what you understand them to be saying.
Leviticus 1:1-17:

Deuteronomy 18:18,19; 31:9-13:

Jeremiah 1:1-19:

II Thessalonians 2:13:

II Timothy 3:14,17:

II Peter 3:16:

> **The Bible-our foundation:**
> Since the Bible is so important to Christianity and its foundation, it is very important that your student come away from this section with a very strong and clear grasp of the Bible's validity. Please make sure to discuss these concepts extensively with your student. Also, you might make them aware of some of the writings and other resources available to them for their understanding of this concept. R.C. Sproul's audio tape series *Hath God Said?* is an excellent resource, as is Josh McDowell's *Evidence that Demands a Verdict* and a handful of other books and tapes. These resources may not be appropriate for the age group your student is currently in, but they may be useful for your explanation of this material, or for your student at a later point. It is important that your student understand that such resources are available to them.

What does Jesus say about the Bible? Look up the following sets of verses, and write down what you understand them to be saying.
Matthew 5:18; 24:35:

John 10:35:

Section 4: The Bible, part 2

In the Church, we talk about the whole Bible being inspired by God, and about the Bible being infallible, or "not able to fail." This means that the writing of every part of the Bible is inspired by, or directed by, God. God gave His words to the human authors so that when they wrote the books that make up the Bible, they wrote only what God wanted them to write, and they wrote everything God wanted them to write. This also means that, like God, the Bible is not able to fail — what it says is never wrong, and it is always everything that needs to be said. The Bible, as God's word, is all that we need for our growth and development as Christians.

Discuss These Questions With Your Parents:

How do we know that the whole Bible is inspired by God?

> Students should understand that the Bible is inspired by God, and that the influence of man on its content is absent. There is no part of what we call the Bible today –the 66 books of the Old and New Testaments – that was added outside of God's control, nor is there anything that is missing from his complete Word. Although they were not taking dictation, the men who wrote the Bible were used of God to express precisely what He desired.

How do we know that the Bible is infallible— unable to fail?

> Students should understand how the Holy Spirit made certain (and continues to make certain) that the Bible, in the original texts, contains no mistakes. God cannot lie, and His Word therefore could contain only truth.

What is the Bible useful for in our lives? How can we use the Bible to understand God?

> You may want to discuss the origins of the Bible with your students. If so, the church can help you with resources to explain the canon and its foundation.

Why do we consider the Bible to be a solid foundation for our faith? What do you believe about the Bible?

Section 5: How God relates to us

Everyone is in a relationship with God. There is no one that you know, and no one in the world, who does not have a relationship with God. Here's the key question: is each relationship a right relationship, or a wrong one? Your relationship with God is important, and you should know whether or not it is a right or wrong relationship.

What makes a relationship with God a right relationship? That's a good question. The answer is in the Bible—that is part of why it is important that we understand the value and truth of the Bible. If what the Bible says is true, then what the Bible says about our relationship with God is also true. So what does the Bible say about our relationship with God?

Begin with Romans 1:18-32. What does this text say about man, and how man and God relate?

> **Man's wayward path:**
> On this page we begin to discuss man, and the fall of man. It significant for your student to understand that they are sinners, and like all other people they are sinful even if they were somehow able to "do no wrong".

What things do you know about yourself, and others, that affects your relationship with God according to these verses?

> It is also important to discuss sins of omission - that is, failing to do all that is required of us, such as worshiping God – as well as sins of commission - that is, things that we do that are not right.

Read Genesis chapter 3. How did the world get this way?

> You might begin with a discussion about the fall and original sin – but make sure that your student understands that because Adam was a divinely appointed representative; he represented you and your student and all others, and that all are sinful because of it.

In what condition do we say that the world is, because of these verses? What parts of the world are not considered to be in this condition?

> Ownership of sin is the first and most important step to certainty of a valid faith. The Westminster Shorter Catechism may again prove a valuable resource for this discussion, especially questions # 39, 82, and 84.

Lesson 1 Summary

We've come a long way this week! Let's look back over what we've learned and write down a few summaries about it.

What is Faith? Of the "heroes of the faith," who did you learn the most from? Why?

Why is it important to have a strong foundation for our faith? What is that foundation?

What two words do we use to describe the Bible? What do they mean? How do we know that these words accurately describe the Bible?

What condition is the world in right now? Why is it in that condition? Does man know that God exists?

Let's memorize a verse from the Bible to close this week out: it's one of the ones that you looked up during your study. Memorize II Timothy 3:16.

Lesson 2: Understanding Your Faith
Up Close and Personal

In this lesson, we'll look at different things about your own faith, and the faith of other people that you know, like your parents or other members of the church. We'll continue to talk about the world we live in, and how God relates to it. We'll also look at the basics of the Gospel, and discuss salvation, which is the result of the faith that we discussed last week.

Section 1: God's relationship to the world, continued: God's righteousness

Man is sinful—that is, he is not able to always do everything that is good and right. Remember in section 5 last week, we talked about how the whole world is "fallen" and is affected by sin, and how all people are considered sinful or unable to do what is right.
How does this change how we relate to God? Let's find out.

Read Genesis 2:15-17. What did God command? What did Adam do, in spite of God's command?

What would happen if God did not keep His word? Would God be a god who we could trust? What must happen in response to Adam's disobedience if God is to remain "just"-that is, trustworthy?

Read Romans 6:23. Is the same thing true for us today? What are "wages?" What wages have you, and everyone around you, earned?

> **God's Justice**
> Here you will return to the trustworthiness of God's word— and consequently, the absolute need for some form of punishment for those who do not keep His commands. You will also review the idea of sin, particularly your student's sin, and how they are guilty, deserving the "wages of sin". Again, be sure to emphasize the truth and reality of this as a personal thing, not simply as something we learn about in Sunday School in a generic way. As always, you will find the Westminster Shorter Catechism a useful resource in covering this material. WSC questions 13-19.

Section 2: God's relationship to the world, part 3: mercy and grace

Man is sinful, and deserving of adequate punishment. God is just and trustworthy, and therefore must punish man. But God, in His great love for us, had a plan full of mercy and grace—a plan for our salvation. These are concepts we will focus on today.

What is "mercy?" Discuss this with your parents. What does the word mean? How do we see it in God's plan for our salvation? Read John 3:16-18, and 3:36. How does God maintain both mercy and justice?

> **Mercy & Grace**
> It is important for your student to realize the significance of both mercy – not receiving what we deserve – and grace – getting what we do not deserve – and understanding the differences between the two. Make sure that your student is aware that neither mercy nor grace is a result of what they do, but is completely a work of God's kindness and love toward us.

What is "grace?" Discuss this word with your parents. How do we see God's grace in Jesus? How do mercy and grace work together for our salvation?

> **Jesus our atonement:**
> Jesus had four things that enabled him to be a sufficient atonement for our sin: He was God in the flesh, He lived a sinless life, He died as a sacrifice for us, and He was resurrected that our sacrifice would be a living atonement. These are difficult concepts, and it is important that your student begin to understand their importance in his salvation. Check the WCF chapter 8 and WSC questions 21-28 for more help!

Talk about Jesus, and who he was, with your parents. Why was Jesus the only one who could provide salvation for us? What four things about Jesus' life are needed for that salvation to be complete?

Section 3: Jesus OUR salvation

So, God in His wisdom and love provided a way for man to be saved from His judgment. But, in order for that to happen, there must be an identification with Jesus—we must be adopted into the family of God. If we have faith in God, we will have these things. These two concepts-identification and adoption—will be our topic for this section.

Read Matthew 27:3-5. What does Judas do in this passage? Is what Judas did enough for salvation in Jesus Christ?

> **Our own salvation:**
> Perhaps the most difficult part of understanding salvation, especially with a covenant child who has grown up in the church, is the need for a personal identification with the work of Christ on the cross. The focus of this section is to help your student understand this.

Now read Mark 14:66-72. What was the difference between Peter's response to his own sin and Judas' response? What do we call the response that Peter had? Have you made a similar response for your own sin? Describe that response.

> **Repentance**
> True repentance is not just acknowledging sin like Judas, but it involves grief and sorrow over sin like Peter. However, they should also know that true repentance is a work in the heart by God's hand, and is not something that they can accomplish apart from Him.

Read Galatians 2:20. Discuss this verse with your parents. Do you understand identification with Jesus Christ? Do you have a similar identification as what the apostle Paul describes here? Describe your identification with Jesus Christ.

> **Identification**
> Your student needs to recognize his bond with Christ in a similar way that Paul acknowledges his. Identifying themselves with Christ and realizing that they therefore live for Him is a key part of living faith.

Now read John 1:12-13. Discuss the idea of "believing in him" with your parents. Do you have the right to be called a child of God? What does this mean for you?

> **Adoption**
> Help your students realize their membership in the family of God; part of this is simply encouragement as they prepare to join the church.
>
> Also, by this point you should have an idea of whether your student has a genuine, credible profession of faith. If he does not, please do not proceed with him/her through the rest of this book without discussing it with an elder or member of the church staff. This is very important for the nurturing of his/her faith.

Section 4: What is a testimony?

The word "testimony" is a legal term used by lawyers and in courts. It means "evidence" or "a statement given under oath." When someone has seen something happen that is against the law, they are asked to give testimony about what they saw.

We use the idea of a testimony in the church, too. When someone has seen God at work, then their description of that work is their testimony. A lot of people talk about what they have learned from reading the Bible recently, or about something that they learned from a sermon or Sunday School lesson— those are testimonies. Some people will describe how God has changed their heart about something or someone— that is a testimony.

All Christians have a testimony; if a person has the identification with Jesus Christ that we talked about in the last section— if they have been adopted into the family of God—then they can give testimony to how God was at work in their lives in this way. This testimony is an account of salvation, a description of how a person came to understand that Jesus is their Savior and Lord.

Do you have a testimony? In the last section we discussed how you know if you are a Christian —how to know if you have been adopted into God's family. If you know that you are a Christian, then you have a testimony. This is an important thing to have—you will be asked to give testimony to your salvation in Jesus Christ in order to join the church. We'll spend the rest of this section and all of the next discussing your testimony.

What is your testimony? Discuss with your parents each of the following topics:
- What is your understanding of your need for salvation?
- When did you first understand this need?
- What have you done in response to your understanding of this need for salvation?
- Do you believe that God is at work in your life?
- What are you doing to help your faith to grow?
- What are you doing to put your faith into action?

Make notes here:

> **Your student's testimony:**
> Once you are confident of a real and living faith present in your student's life, help him/her understand how he/she can communicate his testimony to others. This section and the next are designed to help you with that. Make sure they know that there is not a particular format or manner in which they must write it, but simply that they have something to assist them with understanding how to communicate it.

Section 5: Your testimony

It is helpful to have your testimony written down in some form so that if or when you need to remind yourself of God's work in your life, you can do that easily. Your written testimony does not need to be in any special format: you do not need to worry about correct grammar or complete sentences. You can write it as an "outline" or as a poem if you want to, or you can just write it as a letter to yourself or someone else. The important thing is that you try to write it out.

Write out your testimony here.

Lesson 2 Summary

What does it mean for God to be just?

How does God show mercy and grace to us? What significant thing do we have because of that?

What does it mean to have "identification" with Jesus Christ?

How do people become adopted into the family of God?

What is a testimony? Why is it important to understand yours?

This week's memory verse: 2 Corinthians 5:21

Lesson 3: Basic Training

A Look at the Basics of What We Believe

Because you are moving toward joining the church, it is important that you understand the basics of what a presbyterian church believes. As Christians, we call our beliefs theology: that word simply means "the study of God." Understanding the basic theology of the church is essential for all Christians, and that's the purpose of this lesson.

We've already talked about sin, mercy, grace, God's righteousness, and our salvation— these are all a part of theology! If you understand these concepts, then you already know a pretty good amount of theology.

There are some other areas of theology that are important for us to understand: God's covenants with man, justification, and sanctification. These things will be our topics for this lesson.

Section 1: God's covenants with man

You've probably heard this word at some point: covenant. But what is a covenant? A covenant can be defined very simply: it is an agreement that binds or obligates two parties. This is a very common thing— two students agree to meet at the movie theater for a show: this is a covenant. Two adults commit to each other for marriage: this is a covenant. A man signs a contract saying he will work for a certain company or individual: this is a covenant. Anytime two "parties"-that is, two individuals or groups— make some sort of agreement that both are committed to, it can be called a covenant.

When it comes to a covenant with God, things change a little bit. How do they change? Think back over what you have learned so far, and talk this over with your parents. Write your thoughts here.

> **Covenants with God:**
> Because God is trustworthy and always keeps His word, a covenant with Him will always be kept by Him. Make sure that your student understands that God always keeps His covenants. See WCF chapter 7.

Section 2: God's covenants with man, part 2

God has made covenants with mankind over time, and these covenants are important for us to understand. There are two, and they each go by several names; we'll use the most common names. They are: the Covenant of Works, and the Covenant of Grace. Each of these is significant for our faith, so we'll look at each one individually.
Let's turn to the Scriptures to learn about them. You should discuss these questions with your parents as you go through them. We'll start with the Covenant of Works.

Read Genesis 1:26-31. What things did God say about his creation called man? Write down each thing that God said about man.

> **The Covenant:**
> It is important for your student to understand that the only time in which man's salvation was based on his own work – the only time his work could save him – was during the Covenant of Works, which ended with the fall of Adam into sin. Another helpful resource for discussion of the Covenant besides the WCF is O.Palmer Robertson's book *Covenants* which you may borrow from the Pastor or an Elder.

Read Genesis chapter 2. What do we learn about the Garden of Eden? Particularly, what is said about Adam and his wife in the garden?

What responsibilities did Adam and his wife have in order to keep their covenant with God? What would happen to them if they did not keep their responsibilities?

Read Genesis chapter 3. Did Adam and Eve keep their responsibilities? How did their actions effect their covenant with God? Discuss with your parents God's mercy and grace in relation to this covenant.

Section 3: God's covenants with man, part 3

We've talked about the Covenant of Works, now we'll discuss the Covenant of Grace.
Adam and Eve did not keep their covenant with God, and the Covenant of Works was finished. The good news is that God had another covenant. While the Covenant of Works said, "do this and you will live" (see Gen. 2:17, Rom. 10:5), the Covenant of Grace was given to man even though he was unable to keep any command or covenant—simply by God's grace.
Let's discuss it.

What does the term "redemption" mean? Think about what happened during the Covenant of Works, and how that effects you. What need is there for redemption after this?

Read John 3:16,17, and John 10:17,18. What do these sets of verses say about God's plans for the redemption of man?

Discuss the Covenant of Grace with your parents. In your own words, what is the Covenant of Grace?

Because of God's eternal plan to save His elect, the Covenant of Grace is possible. As soon as the Covenant of Works was broken—and man was fallen—the Covenant of Grace became effective, even though it was not stated as such until later in the Scriptures.

Look back over the "heroes of the faith" list. How was God's grace at work in the lives of these people?

Look at Leviticus chapters 4 and 5. What was it that removed the guilt and provided forgiveness for the sins of the Israelites? How did this work?

Read Jeremiah 31:31-34. Discuss with your parents how the covenant mentioned in this passage is a part of the Covenant of Grace. How is this part of the Covenant of Grace fulfilled?

Describe how the two covenants we've studied work together. How has God provided for His people through covenants? What comfort can we know from these covenants?

Section 4: Justification

Here's another word that you may be familiar with: justification. This word is very important for you, because it describes something that may have already happened in your life. Justification is the first part of a two-part process that is the central aspect of our lives as Christians.

If you look at the word justification, you might notice that there are several other words that look or sound similar. What words can you think of that are this way? Discuss with your parents how these words are related to the word justification.

Read Romans chapter 5. What does the apostle Paul say about justification in this chapter? Based on this reading, write what you think justification is in your own words.

Describe what the significance of justification is to a Christian. Has justification occurred in your life? Talk about this with your parents, and write how justification affects you.

> **Justification and Sanctification:**
> It is very important that your student understand the difference between these two significant concepts. Make sure that they understand that justification is the one time act of God's grace to "justify" them from their sin through Christ, while sanctification is the ongoing process of their growth and continued development in faith through God's teaching hand.
> See the WCF chapters XI and XII and the WSC questions 33 and 35 for very helpful resources for this study.

Section 5: Sanctification

If justification is the first part of a two-part process, then sanctification is the second part of that process. While justification happens only once and lasts forever, sanctification is an ongoing activity that does not end until death—at that point, glorification takes over—that's when Christians no longer struggle or have to deal with sin any more.
Sanctification is really great, because it is a way for God to continually care for us as His children, and it enables us to know Him more deeply. Let's look at what sanctification is:

Read Romans chapter 6. In partnership with chapter 5 and justification, what does chapter 6 say about sanctification? Based on your reading in chapter 6, write a definition of sanctification in your own words.

What events and activities occur in your life that are a part of sanctification? Discuss this with your parents, and write your list below.

Lesson 3 Summary

What is a covenant? Name the two covenants we discussed.

What covenants provide for our salvation? How do they do that?

Give a definition of the words justification and sanctification.

What is the difference between justification and sanctification?

Memory verses: Romans 6:14,15

Lesson 4: Why Do We Baptize Babies?

And Other Good Questions...

In the last lesson, we covered the basic theology that the Presbyterian church believes. The concepts of covenants, justification, and sanctification are the building blocks of our theology.

In this lesson, we'll discuss more theology; there are some areas of theology that are particular to Presbyterians, and are sometimes real "hot potato" issues. They are predestination and the sacraments.

Section 1: Predestination

Discuss the word predestination with your parents. What words do you recognize as being similar words to this one? What do those other words mean?

> **Predestination and Election:**
> To some the doctrine of predestination is what defines Presbyterians. In reality predestination is simply a result of a healthy understanding of the sovereignty of God. Discuss the concepts of destiny and destination with your student – these may be more familiar words and ideas for them to start with. Then discuss how the prefix "pre" adds an advance knowledge and intention to the idea of a destination.

Read Romans 8:28-30 and Ephesians 1:3-8. What do these verses say about predestination? Who is predested? What else happens to those who are predestined?

> Also, make sure your student recognizes that this doctrine is found clearly in scripture, not just in the imaginations of the men in our church! If they have been following the lessons thus far, they will see the importance of its presence in Scripture.

Read John 15:16. What does Jesus say that relates to predestination? What does this mean about the salvation that Christians have?

> You simply can not do better for a resource than the WCF; and if you want still more then see the Pastor or an Elder for a copy of John Gerstner's *A Primer on Free Will* and other resources.

Some Christians have a difficult time accepting what the scripture says about predestination. Why do you think this is the case? What might stand in the way of easy acceptance of this concept?

> **Pride and Predestination:**
> The major idea here is man's pride: it is his pride that often prevents him from readily admitting that God is sovereign, and thus his pride that keeps him from acknowledging the work of God's predestination.

Section 2: The Sacraments, part 1

What is a sacrament? The dictionary says it is simply a religious ritual, but it is more than that. A sacrament is something that is representative of God's covenant with His chosen people. In the Old Testament, some of the sacraments were circumcision (see Genesis chapter 17), the Passover (see Exodus 12), and the sacrifices offered (see Leviticus chapters 1-5). For the New Testament, and for the church today, there are two: Baptism and Communion (or the Lord's Supper). We'll look at what these mean, and why they are important. We'll also look at what particular ways of practicing these sacraments are, according to our theology, most true to the Bible.

Read Genesis 17. What was Abraham commanded to do, as a sign of the covenant between him and God? When was he required to do this? What did this mean? Discuss this with your parents.

> **Circumcision and Baptism:**
> The key to teaching this is to show the link between the Old and New Testament as well as our relationship with the Jew and Israel as Christians and the Church.

Read Galatians chapter 2, and 3:26-29. Are we still required to do what Abraham was required to do? Why or why not? Discuss this with your parents.

> In Scripture, the relationship between circumcision and baptism is very clear. You should discuss this with your student extensively, even taking a day or two if necessary. In addition to the WCF chapters 27 and 28, see the Pastor or an Elder for a copy of the booklet by John Sartelle *Infant Baptism*, which is very thorough and easy to follow or Pierre Marcel's book *The Biblical Doctrine of Infant Baptism*. R. C. Sproul has an audio series entitled *What are the Sacraments?* that may prove helpful too.

What happens today to serve as a sacrament in the same way that circumcision did for Abraham? How does this serve as the substitute for circumcision? Discuss this with your parents.

In your own words, describe what baptism is, and what significance it has. Also talk about why we baptize infants as well as adults in the presbyterian church.

Section 3: The Sacraments, part 2

We've talked about baptism, and how it serves as a sacrament. Now let's talk about communion, or the Lord's Supper.

Read Exodus 12:5-13. What was the Passover? What significance did it have for the Israelites? What did it symbolize for them?

Now read Matthew 26:26-29. How does communion replace the Passover for Christians in the New Testament and today? Discuss this with your parents.

> **Communion is significant:**
> No less important is your student's understanding of communion. For some, this is the main reason they desire to take this class and unite with the church – so they may partake of the Lord's Supper. Our goal here is to help them understand the significance of this means of grace.
> It is especially important that you give attention to the caution that the Lord gave the Corinthians regarding taking the sacrament properly – be sure your student understands this. Of course, in order for them to understand it, they must recognize the significance of the whole concept. See WCF chapter 19 and wSC questions 96-97 to round out your study.

Read John 6:48-58 and I Corinthians 11. What do the wine (or grape juice) and bread stand for in communion? What is the purpose of taking communion for Christians today? Discuss this with your parents.

Read I Corinthians 11:27-30 again. What does Paul (the writer) warn Christians about in this passage? What does this tell you about how you should approach the sacraments, especially communion?

In your own words, describe what communion is, and why it is important for Christians.

Lesson 4 Summary

What is predestination? Does it apply to you?

What is a sacrament? How is it significant for Christians?

Why do we baptize babies?

Is the Lord's Supper important?

Memory verse: Galatians 3:28.

Lesson 5: The Church
Isn't It Just a Building?

Since you're working toward joining the church, it is important to think about the different things that make up the church. We've already talked about the church as a place of faith, and we've discussed some of the important theology of the church. In this lesson, we want to take a look at the church itself, in a variety of ways. We'll look at the church as a universal body of people, and as a local institution. We'll look at how the church is involved in the lives of others. And, we'll look at how you fit into the church, and some of the ways you can be involved in the church as a member.

Section 1: The church universal and the church particular

Many people think of the church as a particular place—maybe a building they worship in, or in some cases another place like a clearing by a lake, or a mountainside. Some other people think of the church as an organization, not very different from the Boy Scouts or the YMCA. But is the church only a building, or only an organization? Or is it much more than this?
Let's look to the Bible, and see what it tells us about the church.

Read Hebrews 11:1-12:3. Remember the Heroes of the Faith? What does 12:1 say about them? How does this apply to the church? Discuss the idea of a "universal church" with your parents.

> **WLC Question 64.** What is the Invisible Church?
> Answer: The invisible church is the whole number of the elect, that have been, are, or shall be gathered into one under Christ the head. (Eph. 1:10, 22–23; John 10:16; 11:52.)

Read 1 Corinthians 1:2,3; Galatians 1:2,3; Revelation 2:1,8,12,18; Revelation 3:1,7,14. What do each of these verses have in common? What is different about each? Discuss with your parents the idea of a "particular" church.

> **WLC Question 62.** What is the Visible Church?
> Answer: The visible church is a society made up of all such as in all ages and places of the world do profess the true religion, and of their children.(1 Cor. 1:2; 12:13; Rom. 15:9–12; Rev. 7:9; Ps. 2:8; 22:27–31; 45:17; Matt. 28:19–20; Isa. 59:21; 1 Cor. 7:14; Acts 2:39; Rom. 11:16; Gen. 17:7)
> **WLC Question 63.** What are the Special Privileges of the Visible Church?
> Answer: The visible church hath the privilege of being under God's special care and government; of being protected and preserved in all ages, not withstanding the opposition of all enemies; and of enjoying the communion of saints, the ordinary means of salvation, and offers of grace by Christ to all the members of it in the ministry of the gospel, testifying, that whosoever believes in him shall be saved, and excluding none that will come unto him.(Isa. 4:5–6; 1 Tim. 4:10.; Ps. 115:1–2, 9; Isa. 31:4–5; Zech. 12:2–4, 8–9; Acts 2:39, 42; Ps. 147:19–20; Rom. 9:4; Eph. 4:11–12; Mark 16:15–16; John 6:37)

Section 2: The church ministers to others

What are some of the ways that the church is involved in the world? What are some of the ministries that the church has to those who are a part of it? This section will look at these issues.

List all of the ministries of our church— ways that the church effects the lives of other people- that you can think of. Don't forget to include all sorts of people, of all ages.

> **Church Ministries:**
> Need some help remembering? If you need more information ask the Pastor or an Elder about the different ministries that our church offers and is involved with; they will be able to give you a summary of what the various ministries of our church are.

There are some ministries of the church that work toward sharing the Gospel (which we discussed earlier) with people who do not know the Gospel; we'll call these Outreach or Evangelism ministries. Can you think of any of these in our church? List them here.

There are some ministries which have the purpose of helping people to understand the Bible and what it instructs us to know and do. We'll call these Teaching ministries. Do you know of any of these at our church? List them here.

There are ministries that are for the purpose of helping people who are in need in some way; we'll call these Benevolence ministries. Which of these do you know about in our church? List them here.

Some ministries are there so that people who believe in God can get together and encourage each other as they grow in their understanding of their beliefs. We'll call these Fellowship ministries. Do you know which ones are these? List them here.

Section 3: The church ministers to you

As a member of the church, you will be one part of a large body, both in a Universal Church sense and it a Particular Church sense. How does this work exactly? What part do you have in this body?

Read 1 Corinthians 12:12-31. What does it mean for you to be a "member of the body" as you read about in these verses?

> **Members of the Body of Christ:**
> Here we introduce the idea of Spiritual Gifts, and using our Spiritual Gifts for the glory of God and the strengthening of His church. If you're not familiar with these— or if you'd like to know more about them— you might find Aubrey Malphurs's book *Maximizing Your Effectiveness* a good introduction to spiritual gifts, as well as other ways that God has uniquely designed His people for service.

Do you have a particular role, function, or gift which you can use as a part of Christ's body? How are you using it? Discuss this with your parents.

How do you feel like the church ministers to you? In what ways are you not being ministered to by your church? Which do you think is more—the amount you are ministered to, or the amount that you are involved in using your gifts for the church?

Lesson 5 Summary

What is the Universal Church? How do you fit into it?

What is the Particular Church? How do you fit into it?

Name some of the ministries that you know about in our church. What kinds of ministries are those?

How are you involved in ministry in our church? How are you being ministered to by our congregation?

Scripture Memory: 1 Corinthians 12:12

Lesson 6: Getting Down to Business

The Organization of the Church

What does it mean to be "Presbyterian" anyway? Aren't we all Christians? Why do we need a particular name or label like that? How come our church is organized differently from other churches in town?

The organization of the church is sometimes a complicated thing to understand. We have a very specific structure for it, and that structure may seem like it is just a lot of meetings and committees that don't do anything but talk about the same things. But if we look at the reason why we have this structure, and how it functions, we'll see that it does have a good purpose after all. Further, if we look for words about the organization of a church in the Bible, we'll see that the structure our church is using is very Biblical.

Section 1: Our denomination, other denominations

There are basically three different ways that a church can be organized or "governed"—the Episcopal system, the Congregational system, and the Presbyterian system. Let's look at each of those:

Episcopal:
> Churches that are governed in this way have one man, or sometimes a group of men, who makes all of the decisions regarding how the church is to be run; he or they tell the people that are members of the church what they can and cannot do as church members. This man, or group of men, is appointed to the church; the church doesn't get to choose who it will be. Each individual church is a part of a larger group of churches that works the same way—there is a man or group of men that make the decisions for the whole denomination.

Congregational:
> These churches do not have a particular person or group of people who make decisions; instead, everyone in the church gets together and votes on what will happen or what will be done. In these churches, the majority rules! Also, the church may or may not belong to a denomination, but if they do belong to one, the decisions for the denomination are made in the same way—and they do not necessarily affect the churches that are members of the denomination. Each church can choose what it wants—the denomination cannot tell the churches what they should do.

Presbyterian:
> In these churches, the members of the church elect people to lead them and to make decisions. They choose men who they believe will be wise, and who will represent them fairly. Presbyterian churches are also usually members of denominations, and the leaders in the denominations are also elected.

Do you know any churches that operate under the episcopal form of government? How about the congregational? List any that you know below.

Do you know of any institution, besides the Presbyterian Church in America (our denomination), that operates with a presbyterian form of government? Describe that institution here.

> **Time for a Civics lesson:**
> The U.S. government— especially the legislative branch— was patterned roughly after the presbyterian form of government. You might talk with your student about how the two are similar: both exercise a representative form of government whereby an elected individual represents the interests of all of those who elected him, and is accountable to them for representing those interests. Just like the legislature, most churches have defined terms for Ruling Elders, and they must be re-elected to serve and lead in that capacity.

Section 2: The officers of the church

When we, as Presbyterians, elect men to represent us and make decisions for us, we say that those men hold an office. Therefore, we call them officers of our church. The officers oversee the spiritual and physical needs of the particular church.
We have two specific offices in the Presbyterian Church in America: the office of Elder and the office of Deacon. Each of these offices has a specific role and function, and we're going to look at those roles in this section.

Elders
Elders are also sometimes referred to as "Overseers." Elders have, as the Book of Church Order tells, duties of "government and spiritual oversight of the church, including teaching." This is a very basic definition; there is a lot that goes into the handling of these duties. Let's look at Scripture to see what it's all about.

Read I Timothy 3:1-7 and Titus 1:5-9. What does the Bible say about the things we should look for in an Elder? Write down a list of these things here.

There are two different kinds of Elders in the church: Teaching Elders and Ruling Elders. In the Presbyterian Church in America, we call the Teaching Elders "Pastors." The Bible has specific words about Pastors, in addition to the words about all Elders.

Read I Corinthians 4:1,2 and James 3:1. What does the Bible say that Pastors are? What does it warn about this (in the James verse)?

Why is it so important that we heed the words of the Bible regarding Elders? Discuss this with your parents, and write your thoughts here.

Section 3: The officers of the church, continued...

Deacons

The office of Deacon is also significant in the church; the Book of Church Order describes it as "one of sympathy and service, after the example of the Lord Jesus; it expresses also the communion of saints, especially in their helping one another in time of need." Deacons look after the church in times of need-whether it is someone who is sick, hungry, or homeless. Deacons take care of these needs and more. Let's go to the Bible for insight into the office of Deacon.

Read I Timothy 3:8-13. What are the qualifications of a Deacon? What is different between Deacons and Elders—what duties, qualifications, etc?

Read Acts 6:1-7. Why do we need Deacons—why shouldn't the Elders take care of these needs? Is there a need for both? Write down why, according to the Bible AND according to your thoughts, we need Deacons.

Trustees
The work of our Trustees is also very important, and they too are elected by the church and have the responsibilities for things like buying and selling property for the church, taking care of the buildings and grounds, and general upkeep of all the church properties. The Trustees and the Deacons are all under the authority of the Session (elders), and the congregation. They manage our funds, and write checks, etc.

Section 4: Church governing and membership

Elders Deacons and Trustees meet regularly— in many churches, they meet every month! The officers of our church are very concerned with overseeing the care, spiritual growth, and activities of the church, and they are very involved in what goes on each week at church.

As you work toward becoming a member of the church, the officers want you to understand how they are at work to oversee the church; they have invited you to attend one of their meetings! At this meeting, you can stay as long as you like, watching what goes on and listening to the discussions. Call the church office to find out when this meeting is.

You'll also have the opportunity to talk with some or all of the Elders about joining the church; If you desire to join the church right away, this will be the time to take the next step in the process (going through this class was the first step). They will want to know about your testimony—you'll be glad that we worked through that a few weeks ago!

If you speak with the Elders and share your testimony with them, then you'll be one step away from being a member of the church! The last step is to stand before the congregation and answer a few questions about what you believe. We'll even tell you the questions ahead of time- in fact, they are listed here:

- ✓ Do you acknowledge yourselves to be sinners in the sight of God, justly deserving His displeasure, and without hope save in His sovereign mercy?
- ✓ Do you believe in the Lord Jesus Christ as the Son of God, and Savior of sinners, and do you receive and rest upon Him alone for salvation as He is offered in the Gospel?
- ✓ Do you now resolve and promise, in humble reliance upon the grace of the Holy Spirit, that you will endeavor to live as becomes the followers of Christ?
- ✓ Do you promise to support the church in its worship and work to the best of your ability?
- ✓ Do you submit yourselves to the government and discipline of the church, and promise to study for its purity and peace?

There they are! By this stage, you should be pretty familiar with what those questions are asking you. If you don't understand one of them for some reason, talk with your parents about it! Once you've answered those questions before the church, you'll be a member of the church! Be proud-this is a significant time for you in your life, one that will have more significance as you grow older.

Lesson 6 Summary

What kind of government does our denomination use? What are the other kinds of church government (define them)?

What are the duties of Elders? What kind of Elders are there?

Why do we need Deacons? How are they different from Elders?

What are the 5 questions you will be asked? Can you answer them all with a "yes"?

Scripture memory: Ephesians 4:14,15

www.ingramcontent.com/pod-product-compliance
Lightning Source LLC
LaVergne TN
LVHW081355060426
835510LV00013B/1839